Things to Say & Not to Say to Parents of a Child with Down Syndrome

A How-To Guide By

Dodi Williams

CONTENTS

Acknowledgments   i

1   Preface   1

2   Strengths   2

3   Conditions   4

4   Life   6

5   Signs   8

6   Congratulations   10

7   Adventures   12

8   Perceptions   14

9   Age   16

10   Image   18

11   Normal   20

12   Different   22

13   Parent   24

14   First Person   26

15   Inclusion   28

ACKNOWLEDGMENTS

I truly enjoy being a parent to my two boys. Evan has been a terrific tour guide into the world of Down syndrome. Alex has been a charming brother to Evan and delights in his accomplishments. I thank my boys and my amazing husband for daily inspiration.

Thanks to my friend, Jessie, who took some of the photos of Evan in this book over the past several years. She has true talent.

PREFACE

Do you want to know how to be informed about Down syndrome without coming across as insensitive? Most parents love to brag on their kiddos. However, parents of children with Down syndrome don't want to immediately become defensive because of tactless questions or statements. Here are some ways to engage in positive conversation and learn more about awesome children with Down syndrome.

Keep in mind that not all parents react the same way. Some may be very sensitive to the topic, while others want to share their knowledge with the world. Be open and receptive to their point of view or conversation style. Do not force conversation if the parent is uncomfortable talking about their child.

The following "Dos" and "Don'ts" are generalizations based on personal experience. Prepare to be educated.

STRENGTHS

Don't say: Is he high-functioning or low-functioning?

Children with Down syndrome are all different, similar to neuro-typical children. Some children are strong in reading, others are great in sports. Each child has his own abilities that sets him apart. Some children take a while to meet a milestone, but can exceed expectations in other areas. Some are social, some are not. The key is to not have any set expectations!

<u>Do</u> say: What are his strengths? What goals are you working towards?

Parents of children with Down syndrome often love to share their children's strengths and accomplishments. This is no different than any other parent. One phrase we like to say is "more alike than different."

CONDITIONS

Don't say: Is it a mild case? Will he outgrow it? Is there a cure?

Down syndrome is caused by an extra chromosome 21. It is a genetic condition that is caused when the embryo is being formed. Geneticists say there are three main variations of Down syndrome. The first is called trisomy 21 which means an extra copy of chromosome 21 is in every cell. This is the most common type. Mosaicism occurs when an extra copy of chromosome 21 is only in some cells. Translocation is the third type, and it means these folks have only part of the extra chromosome 21 in every cell. The variations of these types can affect the individuals differently. As with all children, each child with Down syndrome is unique and may have different abilities or struggles. It is not a disease. It is not contagious. It cannot be a mild case. The child will not outgrow it. There is not a cure because it's not a disease.

Do say: He's so cute! Has he had any health issues?

Children with Down syndrome can have mild to severe health-related issues. One common mild issue may be hypothyroidism. One of the major issues may be heart defects; 40% of children with Down syndrome have a heart defect. The ear canals can be narrower than in neuro-typical children so ear infections are more prevalent; 90% of children with Down syndrome will have a severe ear infection by age 2, which may affect their hearing. The size of adenoids and tonsils can cause obstruction issues or chronic infections because their mouth is typically smaller. Many of these health issues are treatable, so most people with Down syndrome can lead healthy lives. Complimenting children with Down syndrome and asking about their well-being are great ice breakers in learning more about them.

LIFE

Don't say: What's his life expectancy?

The average life expectancy in a person with Down syndrome is around 60 years old. They can live active, healthy lives well beyond 60 years old. However, if a new mom has a neuro-typical child, asking this question would seem absurd. Do not ask morbid questions.

<u>Do</u> say: How's he doing?

Children with Down syndrome may be learning to walk, talk, navigate school, or apply life skills. Instead of focusing on the end of life, focus on the current life, including hopes and dreams.

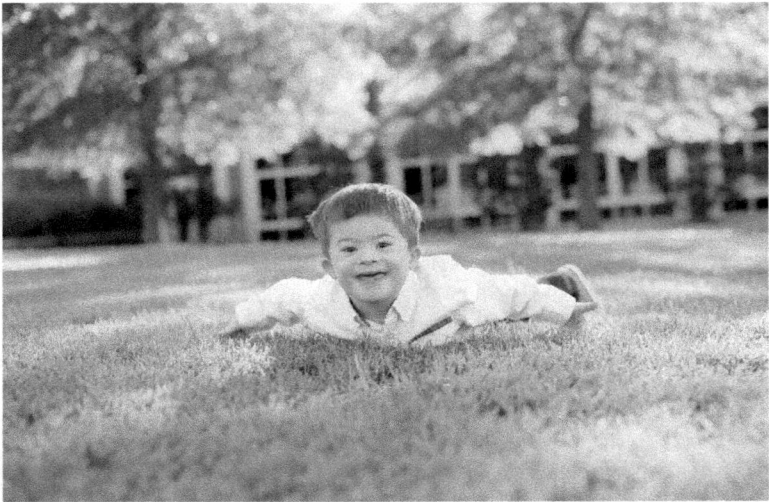

SIGNS

Don't say: Was the test accurate?

Geneticists use a blood test to determine the type of Down syndrome. Do not plant unwarranted doubt or suspicion.

<u>Do</u> say: What kind of signs indicate your child has Down syndrome?

Doctors identify Down syndrome through various indicators both in utero and after birth. Some physical signs may include:

❖ A flattened facial profile and nose
❖ A single, deep, crease across the palm of the hand
❖ A deep groove between the first and second toes
❖ Upward slanting eyes, often with a skin fold that comes out from the upper eyelid and covers the inner corner of the eye
❖ Small, low set ears
❖ Short neck with excess skin at the back of the neck

Not all children with Down syndrome will express these symptoms. They carry genetic tendencies to resemble their parents, just like neuro-typical children.

CONGRATULATIONS

Don't say: Didn't you have the test to find out before he was born?

Prenatal testing comes in many forms and accuracies, and it is a personal choice for many. Asking this type of question has an underlying tone of shame.

<u>Do</u> say: How did you find out your little one had
Down syndrome?

Some diagnoses are made while in utero, and
some are birth diagnoses. Some doctors deliver the
news appropriately, and some need more education.
Pity and sorrow should not be the primary
sentiments offered. Congratulations along with
offering facts, information, and support are the best
approaches to any new or expecting parents.

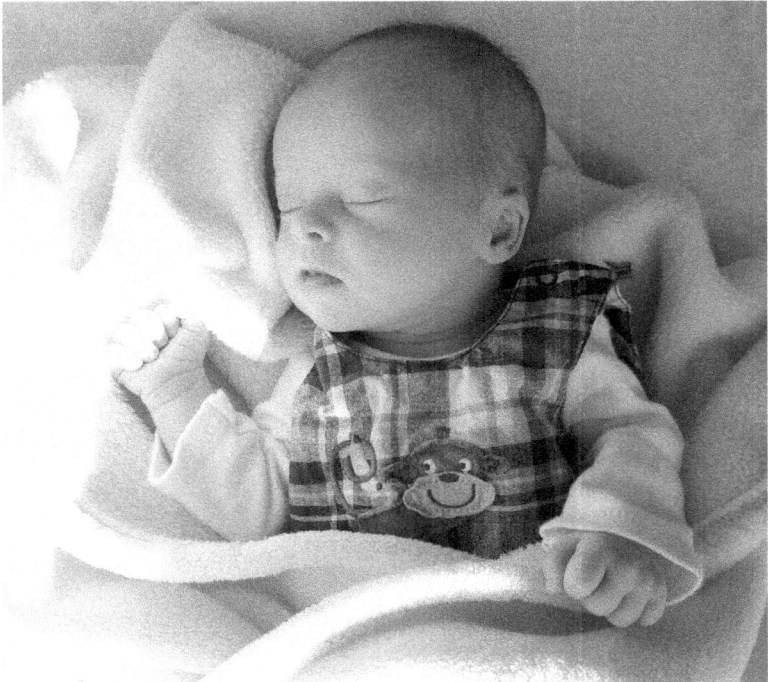

ADVENTURES

Don't say: I'm sorry.

Most people are at a loss for words and use this phrase when they do not know how to express appropriate sentiment. There is nothing sorry about traveling down an unexpected path and finding light, hope, and love in a world full of inspiration and different perspectives.

<u>Do</u> say: It sounds like you are in for an interesting
adventure.

Child-rearing in itself is an adventure. Discussing
the different routes and speeds of the adventure can
lead to healthy and positive outlooks.

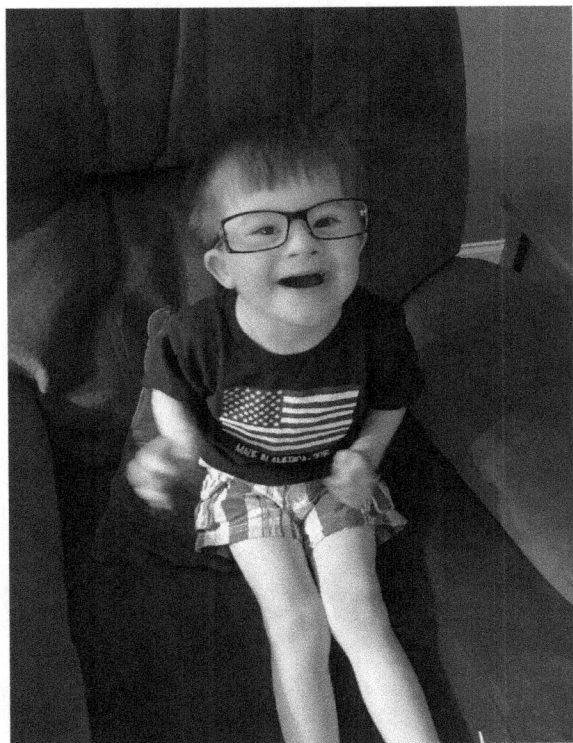

PERCEPTIONS

Don't say: He will always be happy!

Children with Down syndrome express a wide array of emotions. They may be happy, scared, angry, frustrated, stubborn or more.

<u>Do</u> say: He's doing a great job!

Compliment the child on the good things the child is doing. Children love praise and recognition for a job well done.

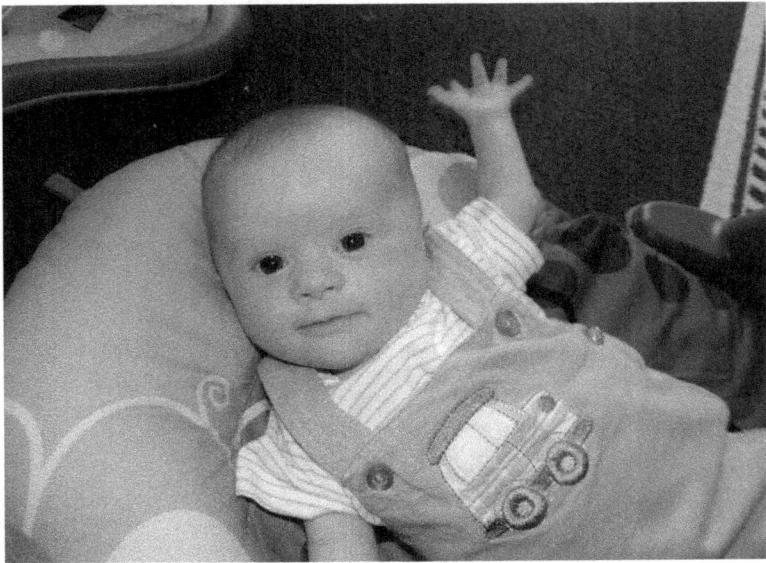

AGE

Don't say: He will be a baby forever.

Children with Down syndrome relate with their peers in all stages of life. Their thoughts and feelings will be similar to others. It may take them a bit longer to achieve milestones, but they will get there. Some marry, drive, and have productive jobs.

<u>**Do**</u> **say:** What are his interests?

Focus on the child, not the condition. Children with Down syndrome have a wide array of interests just like their neuro-typical peers.

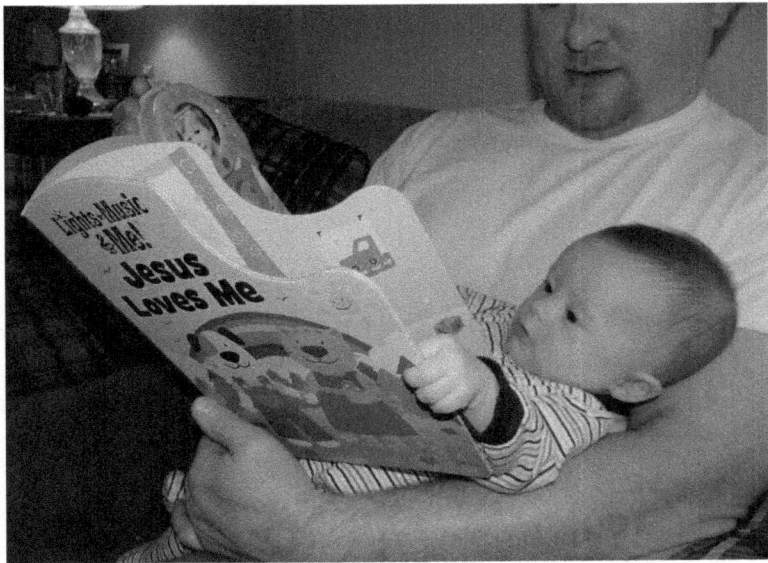

IMAGE

Don't say: He doesn't look like he has Down syndrome.

Children are all unique. These phrases have an underlying tone of dismissiveness or inaccuracies about the diagnosis. Many children have conditions that are not always visible.

Do say: Your child is beautiful.

Give compliments or flattery as you would toward any neuro-typical child.

NORMAL

Don't say: What's wrong with him? Is he normal?

There is nothing wrong with children that have Down syndrome. They do not suffer from a disease. It is a condition or syndrome that may cause cognitive delays. Down syndrome occurs in 1 out of 700 births in the U.S., so yes, they are normal.

<u>Do</u> say: How is your child affected?

Each child with Down syndrome may be affected differently. Most children with Down syndrome will grow up and lead healthy and productive lives. Instead of saying normal, use the term typical or neuro-typical.

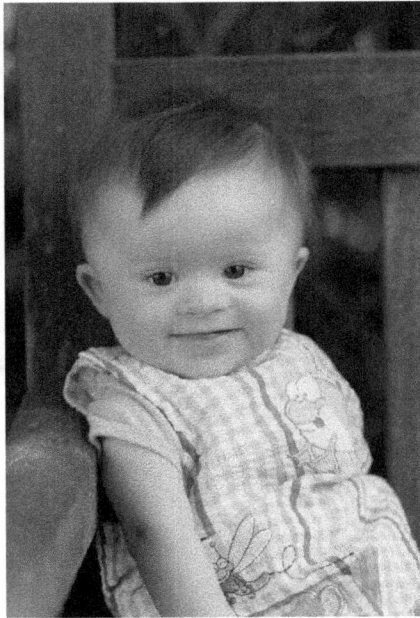

DIFFERENT

Don't say: Is your child mentally retarded?

The "r" word is a derogatory outdated term. It can be offensive to many. Do not use it.

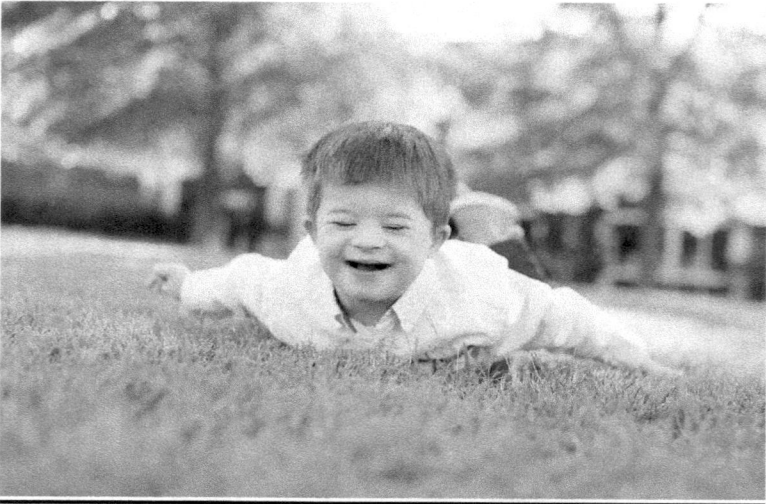

Do say: How is your child differently abled?

Do not focus on the disability, but on the different abilities. Cognitive and intellectual delays may be apparent but each child may experience them differently. This will not deter from the fact that each child has many strengths and talents. Never underestimate a child with Down syndrome. Remember, children with Down syndrome are far more alike than different from neuro-typical children.

PARENT

Don't say: You must be special to be his parents.

Having a child with Down syndrome does not promote a parent to a superior status. Parents of a child with Down syndrome are regular people that have embarked on a journey with a fabulous tour guide.

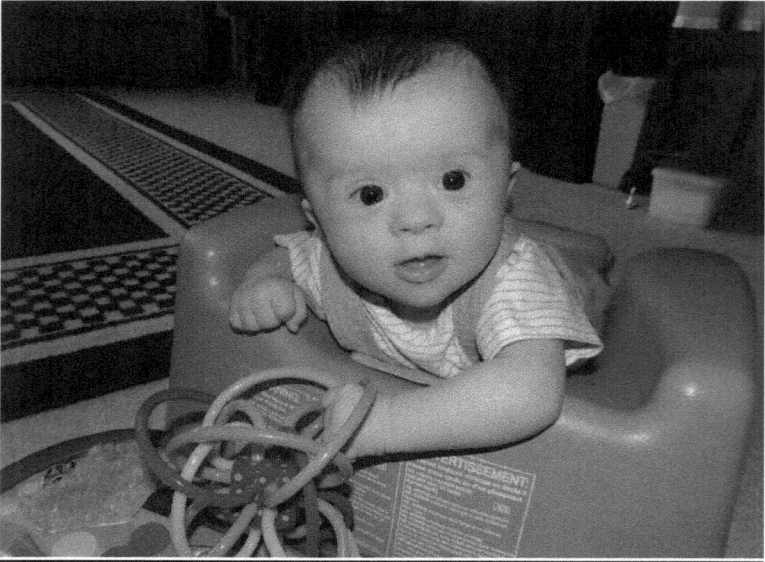

<u>Do</u> say: You're doing a great job, parent.

Take note of the parent that becomes an advocate for their children. Encourage them and lift them up along the way.

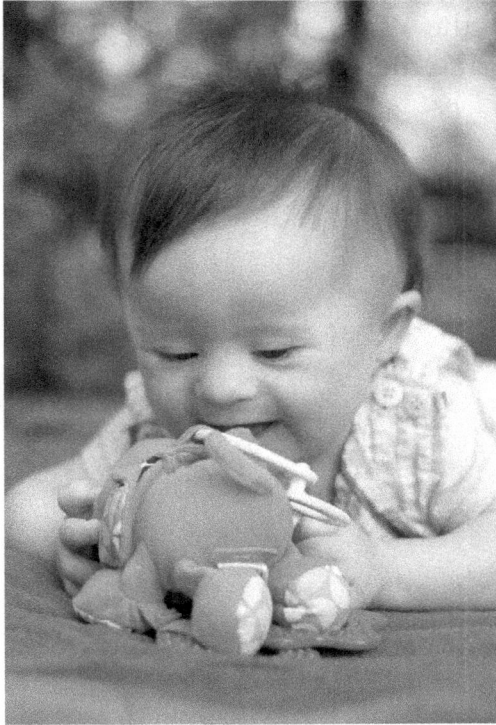

FIRST PERSON

Don't say: He's a Down's child.

Don't put the diagnosis before the child. The name of the condition is Down syndrome. No apostrophe is used. Dr. John Langdon Down provided the first formal description of the syndrome and therefore no possessive is used.

<u>Do</u> say: He has Down syndrome.

Each child should be respected as a person first, before their condition. However, if Down syndrome is not relevant to the conversation, there is no need to bring it up. Many parents will abbreviate Down syndrome to DS in written form.

INCLUSION

Don't say: Shouldn't he be in an institution?

Institutions were the norm 50 years ago, which wasn't that long ago. However, parents no longer institutionalize children with Down syndrome.

<u>Do</u> say: How is school going?

Schools provide children with Down syndrome various options in education. These children make tremendous strides and progress when included in typical school environments. Each parent makes a choice in the level of inclusion based on the child's needs and abilities. Inclusive environments promote diversity, kindness, and friendship. Each child is unique and may require different levels of assistance or accommodations. Each decision can be difficult for parents to make so do not judge them. Offer support and encouragement as they advocate for their child.

ABOUT THE AUTHOR

Dodi Williams lives in South Carolina with her husband and two young sons, one of whom has Down syndrome and autism. She is a full-time data analyst, a part-time avid baker and a part-time hopeful writer.

www.ingramcontent.com/pod-product-compliance
Lightning Source LLC
Chambersburg PA
CBHW060646030426
42337CB00018B/3476